WEL
HOC

Pavel **Bure**

KERRY BANKS

GREYSTONE BOOKS
Douglas & McIntyre Publishing Group
Vancouver/Toronto/New York

Greystone Books
A division of Douglas & McIntyre Ltd.
2323 Quebec Street, Suite 201
Vancouver, British Columbia
Canada V5T 4S7
www.greystonebooks.com

National Library of Canada Cataloguing in Publication Data
Banks, Kerry, 1952–
    Pavel Bure
    (Hockey heroes)
    ISBN 1-55054-920-0

    1. Bure, Pavel—Juvenile literature. 2. Hockey players—Biography—Juvenile literature. I. Title. II. Series: Hockey heroes (Vancouver, B.C.)
GV848.5.B87B29 2002   j796.962′092   C2002-910027-5

Editing by Michael Carroll
Cover and text design by Peter Cocking
Front cover photograph by Jim McIsaac/Bruce Bennett Studios
Printed and bound in Hong Kong by C&C Offset Printing Co. Ltd.
Printed on acid-free paper ∞

We gratefully acknowledge the assistance of the Canada Council for the Arts, the British Columbia Arts Council, and the Government of Canada through the Book Publishing Industry Development Program (BPIDP) for our publishing activities.

Photo credits

Photos by Bruce Bennett Studios:
pp. i, 9, 41, 43: Jim McIsaac
pp. iii, iv, 10, 22, 25, 33, 34, 37, 38: Bruce Bennett
pp. 18, 29: Art Foxall
p. 38: Jim Leary

Photos by Tass:
pp. 3, 7: Utkin
p. 4: Soloviev

Photo by the *Vancouver Sun:*
p. 13: Ralph Bower

Photos by the Vancouver Canucks:
pp. 14, 17, 21: Vancouver Canucks
p. 26: Kent Kallberg
p. 30: Jeff Vinnick

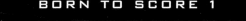

CONTENTS

Pavel Bure is known as

a game-breaker, a player

who scores big goals

that can suddenly turn

games around.

C H A P T E R   O N E

Born to Score

If you were to ask a scientist to design the perfect hockey scoring machine, you would likely get something that looks a lot like Pavel Bure. The Russian winger has all the key ingredients: explosive speed; shifty moves; a hard, accurate shot; and a burning desire to put the puck in the net. As Ray Whitney, a former linemate with the Florida Panthers, once noted: "I've never seen a guy who wants to score more than Pavel. He even keeps stats with our goalies in practice and puts them up on the board to taunt them. He's just so competitive."

But more than simply a scorer, Pavel is also an exciting player, someone who can lift the fans out of their seats with his high-velocity rushes. When he has the puck, anything can happen. And when it does, you better not blink. Because with Pavel everything gets done fast.

It's been that way since he was a child. As his father, Vladimir, recalls, "He was always a very fast boy. It was not possible for him to sit still, even for a minute. *Zoom! Zoom!* Every time, it's 'Where's Pavel? Where's Pavel? Look out, here comes that crazy Pavel.'"

Speed and athletic talent were in Pavel's blood. His grandfather, Valeri, was a member of the Soviet national water-polo team. He later became a swimming coach and helped turn Vladimir into a national champion in the 100- and 200-meter freestyle events. Vladimir competed in three Olympics—1968, 1972 and 1976—winning one silver and three bronze medals.

Vladimir hoped Pavel would follow the family tradition. When Pavel was three months old, his father was already teaching him to dog-paddle in the bathtub. But Pavel's first love was hockey. As a toddler, he ran up and down the halls of his family's Moscow

Big Red Machine

The Soviet Union formed its first hockey league in 1946. Eight years later the Soviets entered a team at the World Championships for the first time and won the tournament, thrashing Canada in the gold-medal game 7–2. Between 1963 and 1988, the Big Red Machine won gold medals at six of seven Winter Olympics and 15 of 18 World Championships. A great deal of this success was due to the early intensive development of young players, such as Pavel Bure (*shown opposite*), who at 12 years old was already a rising star.

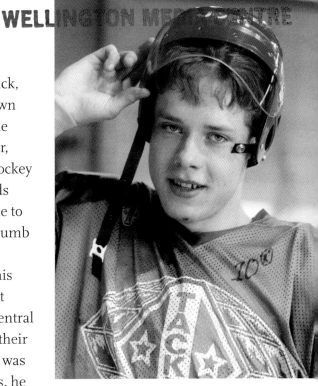

apartment with a tiny plastic stick, imagining he was streaking down the ice. Hockey was a passion he shared with his younger brother, Valeri. They often played ball hockey in the frozen streets with friends after school, too lost in the game to notice their feet were turning numb from the cold.

Pavel was six when he had his first hockey tryout. In the Soviet system all the major teams—Central Army, Dynamo, Spartak   had their own hockey schools. If a player was accepted into one of the schools, he could move up the ranks until he finally reached the top team. Because Vladimir had been a member of Central Army, that was where he took Pavel.

The tryout was a disaster. Pavel's skate blades were dull, and he spent most of the session waddling around on his ankles and clinging to the boards. When the coaches called out the players' names, Pavel was the last picked. After practice Vladimir had a chat with his son. "Look, it is not possible for you to be last. You are a Bure! You must be first! If you want to be a sportsman, then sports must become your life."

Vladimir told Pavel that if he didn't improve in two months he wouldn't get another tryout. Pavel got the message. He

practiced hard, copying the style of the better skaters. Two
months later, when they went back, he wasn't the last. By the
end of the year he was the best.

At age 11 Pavel was one of three players chosen to take part
in the filming of a TV show with Soviet goalie great Vladislav
Tretiak and a visiting Canadian hockey star named Wayne
Gretzky. Little did Gretzky realize that nine years later he would
play against one of the youngsters he skated with that day.

Although Pavel knew about Gretzky, he never imagined playing in North America. At the time Soviet players weren't allowed
to leave the country except to compete in tournaments. Pavel's
dream was to make the national team and win an Olympic gold
medal, the one thing his father had never been able to do.

Vladimir set high standards. One of the rules was that Pavel
had to score a third of his team's goals in every game. Even if
his team scored 12 goals, Pavel had to score four. A hat trick—
three goals—wasn't good enough.

Because Vladimir was a swimming champion,
the Bures lived well by Russian standards. They
had money for nice clothes and a car and could
afford annual vacations. But that changed in 1979
when Vladimir retired and became a swim coach,
which didn't pay as well. In the early 1980s,

Pavel starred at

the 1989 World Junior

Championships.

Pavel's parents separated. Vladimir moved out and Tatiana, his
mother, had to find work. Times were tough, and Pavel thought
he might have to quit hockey to work full-time. But Tatiana told
him to follow his dream.

At 14 Pavel made the Central Army junior team and began to earn some money. A year later, in 1986, he visited Canada with a touring Soviet midget team. When the squad played in Edmonton, Pavel and his teammates got autographs from Gretzky and two other Edmonton Oilers: Paul Coffey and Kevin Lowe. It was the highlight of the trip.

A year later Pavel was promoted to the Central Army senior team, the strongest club in Russia. It was coached by Viktor Tikhonov, who also coached the national team. Tikhonov put Pavel on a line with two other fast-skating teenagers: Alexander Mogilny and Sergei Fedorov. The flashy trio made their international debut at the World Junior Championships in Anchorage, Alaska, in December 1989, and led the Soviet team to the gold medal.

Vladimir Bure trained Valeri and Pavel to be world-class athletes.

Although Pavel was two years younger than most of the players in the tournament, he topped all Soviet scorers with eight goals and six assists, and was voted the best forward in the competition. Pavel was thrilled. Even Vladimir was impressed. "You're almost there," he told his son, "but it's another step to the national team."

Pavel proved his worth in his first full season with Central Army, scoring 17 goals and nine assists in 32 games and winning the 1989–90 rookie-of-the-year award. That same season he also played in the World Junior tournament in Finland, winning a silver medal. A few months later he made his initial appearance on the Soviet national team at the 1990 World

Championships in Switzerland and took home a gold medal. As a reward, all of the players were given us$10,000. Pavel used his money to buy a Lada, his first car.

As Pavel was climbing to the top of his game, things were changing in the Soviet Union, where the Communist political system was tottering. Sensing it wouldn't be long before Soviet players would be allowed to play in North America, National Hockey League team managers began drafting young Russians. At the 1989 Entry Draft the Vancouver Canucks picked Pavel in the sixth round.

It was a risky move because most people believed Pavel hadn't played enough senior-level games to be eligible for the draft. When other teams complained, the league investigated.

NHL president John Ziegler first ruled that Pavel was ineligible, but after the Canucks appealed and presented their evidence, he changed his mind and said they could keep Pavel's rights.

In the summer of 1989, for the first time, the Soviets allowed a few veteran players to leave to play in the NHL. Igor Larionov and Vladimir Krutov joined the Canucks, Sergei Makarov went to the Calgary Flames, and Viacheslav Fetisov joined the New Jersey Devils. But some young players also began leaving. After the 1989 World Championships in Sweden, Mogilny secretly flew to New York, where he signed with the Buffalo Sabres. In July 1990, just before the Goodwill Games in Seattle, Fedorov slipped away from the Soviet team and signed with the Detroit Red Wings.

Worried that Pavel would be the next to go, Soviet hockey officials demanded he sign a contract that would force him to stay in Russia until 1994. When Pavel refused, Tikhonov dropped him from the national team when it left to play in the 1991 Canada Cup that August. The move backfired.

THE PAVEL BURE FILE

Position: Right wing

Born: March 31, 1971, Moscow, Russia

Height: Five foot ten inches (1.78 meters)

Weight: 189 pounds (86 kilograms)

Shoots: Left

Number: 10

Nicknames: The Russian Rocket, Pascha

Favorite Cars: Mercedes, Ferrari

Favorite Stick: Easton Synergy

Favorite Subject in School: History

Hobbies: Travel, tennis, reading

Possible Career After Hockey: Politics

Childhood Hockey Heroes: Valeri Kharlamov, Boris Mikhailov

Hockey Highlights: First NHL game; playing in 1994 Stanley Cup finals

Pavel took the NHL by storm as a rookie, thrilling fans with his fancy stickhandling and high-speed, end-to-end rushes.

CHAPTER TWO

Rocket Launch

A week after the Soviet team left for Canada, Vladimir Bure and his two sons boarded a plane and flew to Los Angeles. Tatiana followed later. It was a big decision because they didn't know if they'd ever be able to return to Russia. Upon arrival, the Bures visited Ron Salcer, an NHL player-agent. They wanted Salcer to represent them in contract talks with the Canucks.

Pavel hoped to sign with Vancouver right away, but the Canucks first had to work out a deal with the Central Army team, which still owned his playing rights. While they waited,

Pavel and Valeri worked out under Vladimir's watchful eye at a local rink. Although Pavel had yet to play a single NHL game, he was already a figure of intense curiosity. A photographer even showed up to take his picture for a hockey card.

The dispute lasted nearly two months before the Canucks settled the issue with a transfer fee of US$250,000 to Soviet hockey officials. Vancouver then inked Pavel to a four-year deal worth US$2.7 million. His signing created a stir in the hockey-crazed city, where fans had endured 15 straight losing seasons. If the press reports were accurate, this young Russian might be the player who could turn things around.

Pavel attended his first practice in Vancouver on November 2, 1991, at a small arena in the city's east end. Normally such public practices attracted only a couple of dozen fans. This time a thousand curious onlookers showed up. When the Canucks' staff began handing out publicity photos of Pavel, there was a near-riot to get the souvenirs.

Pavel played his first NHL game against the Winnipeg Jets on November 5. The Pacific Coliseum was sold out. Everyone had come to get a look at this mysterious, blue-eyed kid from Moscow. They got their money's worth. Although he

Bodywork

Although Pavel Bure isn't big by NHL standards, he's very strong. His body was built by years of training with his father, Vladimir, who put him through intense summer workouts to boost his strength, stamina and flexibility. The routines involved running and stretching exercises, weight lifting, basketball, soccer, tennis and swimming. Geoff Courtnall, one of Pavel's former Vancouver Canucks teammates, once watched as Vladimir forced Pavel to run a series of 20 100-meter dashes, with only a 10-second break for each one. "It almost made me puke just watching him," Courtnall said.

didn't score, Pavel thrilled the hometown fans with his dash and daring. He made three sensational rushes during the match, bursting through the Jets' defense at warp speed. Tom Larscheid, the commentator on the Canucks' radio broadcast that night, remembers the roar of the crowd rising in volume as Pavel took the puck and raced toward the Jets' net: "He literally lifted people out of their seats. I'd never witnessed anything like that at the Coliseum. The atmosphere was electric."

Asked by reporters for his thoughts after the game, Pavel said, with the aid of an interpreter, "It was very exciting. I will remember this day all my life. It was beautiful." Local sportswriters were just as enthusiastic. Archie McDonald of the *Vancouver Sun* declared: "Bure raised goose pimples so big you could scrape carrots on them." Iain MacIntyre, another *Sun* writer, asked: "If Winnipeg are the Jets, then what do you call Pavel Bure? How about the Rocket? It fits Bure perfectly. He is the fastest Soviet creation since *Sputnik*." The nickname stuck. Soon everyone was calling him the Russian Rocket.

Under the direction of general manager and coach Pat Quinn, Vancouver had been slowly improving, but Pavel speeded up the process. By the end of January, the Canucks led the Smythe Division. Playing with crafty center Igor Larionov and hardworking left winger Greg Adams, Pavel was a constant threat. After a loss to Vancouver, New Jersey Devils coach Tom McVie said about Pavel: "This kid is frightening. I thought Fedorov was fast, but this kid is even faster. He's one of the best young players I've seen in a long, long time."

As easy as Pavel was making it look on the ice, life away from the rink was more difficult. He spoke little English and was often homesick. The travel was tiring, the food odd, and the intense media attention confusing. It was also hard to adjust to the reaction from the fans. "It is very strange," he told one interviewer. "Many times I talk to my friends in Moscow on the phone. I tell them that 16,000 people cheer for me. They don't believe me. It is unbelievable."

So many screaming teenage girls began waiting for him outside the Coliseum that the team had an usher retrieve

Pavel has the soft, quick hands of a natural goal scorer.

Pavel's Dodge Stealth from the parking lot and drive it inside the building. After games he would go directly from the dressing room to his car. Then, when the gate was raised, he'd drive out like Batman bursting from the Bat Cave in his Batmobile.

Vancouver finished first in its division and second overall in the Western Conference, setting new team records for points (96) and wins (42). Pavel tied the club's rookie record for most points with 60, and despite playing only 65 games, led Vancouver with 34 goals.

The Canucks were expected to defeat Winnipeg in the first playoff round, but the Jets nearly pulled off an upset, shutting down Pavel's line and taking three of the first four games. However, the Russian Rocket shook loose to score seven points in the next two games and Vancouver came back to win the series.

The fairy tale came to an end in the next round against the Edmonton Oilers. The Oilers gave pesky winger Esa Tikkanen the job of covering Pavel, and he performed it perfectly, hooking him, knocking him down and tugging on his sweater. The Canucks went down to defeat in six games.

Although the season ended on a sour note, there was a sense of hope in Vancouver. The club had made great strides, and Pavel, who was voted the NHL's rookie of the year, had given the team something it had never had before: a game-breaker. As Quinn noted about his Russian rookie, "I watch him every day and he's not just a kid with skill, but a kid with determination and a work ethic. The best thing is, I think, is that's he's only going to get better."

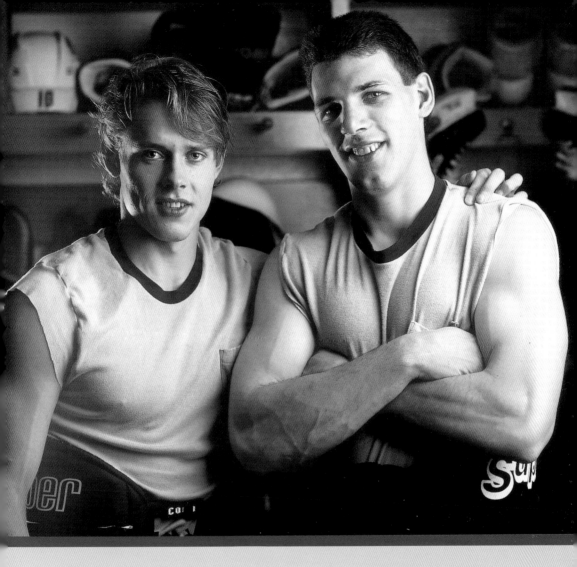

THE ODD COUPLE

When Pavel Bure joined the Vancouver Canucks, he spent a lot of time hanging out with winger Gino Odjick, a Native player from Quebec. Physically they made an unusual pair. Pavel is short and blond with soft, angelic features, while Gino is a big, dark, tough-looking guy, who gets involved in a lot of rough stuff on the ice. Despite their differences, the two hit it off. The friendship continued after they left Vancouver. In 1998, when Gino's wife gave birth to a son, they named him Bure Odjick.

It has been said that

when Pavel sees the

blueline he smells blood.

He never lets up near

the net.

CHAPTER THREE

The Breakaway Kid

Pavel Bure's terrific rookie season had raised expectations. Some fans predicted he'd score 50 goals in 1992–93. That was asking a lot. Only four NHLers had hit the 50-goal mark the year before. But Pavel was ready to try. He reported to training camp in the best condition of any of the Canucks' players, having added several pounds of muscle to his upper body.

The Muscovite got off to a fast start. In an 8–1 rout of Winnipeg, he fired four goals past goalie Bob Essensa, three of them in a 12-minute span. After 20 games, he had scored 20 goals and his whirlwind rushes were becoming a regular feature on the TV highlight reels. Most players rarely got a breakaway, but Pavel seemed to bust free every night.

By New Year's Day, the Canucks were cruising in first place. They went unbeaten in 18 straight home games before finally losing to the defending Stanley Cup champion Pittsburgh Penguins. Despite playing with a variety of different linemates, Pavel was proving tough to stop. After watching the Russian buzz through his team's defense, Minnesota North Stars general manager Bob Gainey declared: "I don't know if you can get any quicker and stay within the boards. If he's having a big night, then we're not going to."

Pavel's popularity continued to increase. Letters poured in by the box load. When he returned from one road trip, 26 pounds (12 kilograms) of mail were waiting for him. The Canucks' souvenir stores were now selling Bure jerseys, T-shirts, posters, hats, school binders and pajamas. Packs of girls began following him home after games and gathering outside of his downtown condo. Eventually he had to move out and find a spot in a private apartment complex.

Pavel's film-star looks caught the attention of female fans.

Although Pavel had the most fanatic following, he was only one of a new wave of young European stars that included Teemu Selanne in Winnipeg, Jaromir Jagr in Pittsburgh, Mats Sundin in Quebec, and Pavel's two former Russian linemates, Alexander Mogilny in Buffalo and Sergei Fedorov in Detroit.

Helped by a crackdown on holding and hooking fouls, offense boomed. By the season's end, a record 14 players had scored 50 goals and 20 players had reached 100 points. Pavel collected 60 goals and 50 assists, smashing Patrik Sundstrom's club record of 91 points. Vancouver won its division for the second straight year, but again stumbled in the playoffs, losing in the second round to Gretzky's Los Angeles Kings.

During the off-season, Pavel's agent, Ron Salcer, attempted to open talks on a new contract. NHL salaries were climbing fast; and there were now more than 100 players earning more than Pavel. But no progress was made. Pavel's frustration with the situation increased in December when Mogilny and Fedorov signed new deals with their teams worth US$3 million a year.

Unlike the previous season, the Canucks couldn't put together a winning streak in 1993–94. Bothered by a pulled groin muscle, Pavel started slowly, too. But after the NHL All-Star Game he began to roll. In March he scored 19 goals and 30 points in 16 games and was voted the NHL player of the month. The Russian Rocket finished with 107 points and a league-high 60 goals. He had scored 154 goals in his first three seasons, third most in NHL history behind Mike Bossy and Gretzky.

Although Pavel had come close to matching his previous year's output, the club's other top guns—Trevor Linden, Cliff Ronning, Geoff Courtnall—had all slumped. Few people expected Vancouver to go far in the playoffs. Things looked grim when the Canucks fell behind three games to one against Calgary in the first round. But Vancouver rallied to scratch out two wins in overtime to tie the series. The seventh game in Calgary was a nail-biter. The Flames led 3–2 with four minutes left when Greg Adams scored to send the contest into overtime for the third straight time.

The Russian Rocket

has netted his share

of acrobatic goals.

Calgary had a great chance to win the series, but Vancouver goalie Kirk McLean made a miraculous kick save on Robert Reichel. Then, early in the second period of sudden death, the Canucks got a break. Defenseman Jeff Brown hit Pavel with a long pass at the Flames' blueline. Bure jetted free and went in alone on goalie Mike Vernon. He made a couple of fakes, then tucked the puck into the net between Vernon's right pad and the post. It was the biggest goal in the Canucks' history, and it set off a wild celebration.

Energized by beating the Flames, Vancouver downed the Dallas Stars in five games. In Game 2 of the series, the Russian Rocket played what many felt was his best game as a pro. Besides scoring two goals, he also flattened Dallas tough guy Shane Churla with a flying elbow, a foul that earned him a US$500 fine. Pavel continued his inspired play in the next series as Vancouver defeated the Toronto Maple Leafs and advanced to meet the New York Rangers in the Stanley Cup finals. The powerful Rangers were heavy favorites, but the series was a close one.

After falling behind three games to one, the Canucks roared back to tie the series. The seventh game was played before a noisy crowd at Madison Square Garden. New York won 3–2 and captured its first Cup in 54 years. The Canucks went home bruised and disappointed, but proud of their effort. Pavel scored 16 goals in the playoffs, the most of any player, and racked up 31 points, second only to the Rangers' Brian Leetch.

Two days later 30,000 people showed up at a celebration for the Canucks at Vancouver's BC Place. When Pavel stepped to the microphone, the ovation lasted five minutes. That day the team announced it had signed its 23-year-old shooting star to a five-year contract worth US$25 million. "I never dreamed about something like this," Pavel told reporters. "I'm really excited that I will be spending lots of years here in Vancouver."

BLADE RUNNER

When people discuss the NHL's fastest skaters, Pavel Bure tops the list. The Russian Rocket credits his ability to his coaching as a youth. In Russia the main focus was always on skating drills. Often young players didn't even see a puck for the first 50 minutes of a practice. Although there is no doubt Pavel can really move, his explosive acceleration is even more important than his speed. He can take off in a heartbeat. Says Vancouver Canucks conditioning coach Peter Twist: "Some other players could beat Pavel in a race around the rink, but no one has a quicker first three strides. It's his ability to get up to top speed in a short distance that sets him apart."

Pavel's reluctance to

discuss his private life has

earned him a reputation

as one of the NHL's most

mysterious players.

CHAPTER FOUR

Winters of Woe

As usual Pavel Bure spent the summer in Los Angeles. When he returned to Vancouver in the fall of 1994, he moved into a new home with a swimming pool, a hot tub and a fountain. It seemed as if he was looking forward to a long career on the West Coast. But that perception would soon change.

The enthusiasm created by the Canucks' playoff run was put on hold in October when a feud over salaries between players and owners caused the longest shutdown in NHL history. Half the season was canceled before play began on January 20, 1995.

During the lockout, Pavel returned to Russia for the first time since 1991. Communism had been replaced by democracy, but there was a lot of chaos. Gangs of criminals had taken control of many businesses. When Pavel joined a group of former Soviet stars for an exhibition series against Russian clubs, all the players were given bodyguards and the team traveled with an escort of soldiers.

The Canucks finally reported to camp, but Pavel was still missing. There was a dispute over money. His agent, Ron Salcer, claimed that according to the terms of Pavel's contract the team owed him more than us$1.7 million for lost wages during the lockout. The Canucks disagreed. Pavel's holdout ended after a long-distance phone conversation with his father, but the argument proved trouble was brewing behind the scenes.

The entire season was filled with conflict. Quinn had given up the coaching job to his assistant, Rick Ley, who didn't hit it off with some of the players. When the club had a slow start, the hometown fans, who were already in a cranky mood because of the lockout, started booing. For the first time Pavel found himself attacked in the media.

One of his loudest critics was *Hockey Night in Canada* commentator Don Cherry, who called the young Russian "greedy" and said his large contract had caused hard feelings on the team. On his popular

Numerology

Prior to the 1995–96 season, Pavel Bure changed his uniform number from 10 to 96. Although he never explained why, it's likely Pavel picked the number because it represented the date he arrived in North America. He landed on the sixth of September, or 9/6. After suffering two injury-filled seasons while wearing 96, he switched back to 10 for good.

"Coach's Corner" segment on March 25, Cherry claimed Pavel had threatened to sit out the seventh game of the previous year's playoff series with Calgary unless the Canucks signed him to a contract. Quinn stomped into the TV studio and angrily denied Cherry's charge, insisting Pavel had made no such threat. However, the truth will never be known.

After finishing sixth in their conference, the Canucks upset the St. Louis Blues in the first round of the playoffs. Pavel scored a team-record seven goals and 12 points in the seven-game series, but hopes of another postseason charge ended in the next round as Vancouver was swept by the Chicago Blackhawks.

In 1995–96 the Canucks moved into a new arena called General Motors Place. In a bid to add some scoring pop, the team acquired Alexander Mogilny in a trade with the Buffalo Sabres. It was hoped he and Pavel would re-create their youthful magic, but in the early going the combination fizzled.

On November 9, in Chicago, the Canucks' fortunes took an ugly turn when Pavel hobbled off the ice. He had torn a ligament in his right knee. Surgery was needed, and he would be

gone for the rest of the year. The team never recovered from this setback. In March, Ley was fired and Quinn returned as coach. After scraping into the playoffs by a single point, the Canucks were swiftly eliminated by the Colorado Avalanche.

At training camp before the 1996–97 season, Pavel appeared to have recovered from his surgery. He made several eye-popping rushes in the preseason games and scored a dazzling goal against the Boston Bruins. Bursting in from the wing, he pulled the puck back into his skates, then kicked it forward to his stick and swept the puck past startled goalie Scott Bailey. The replay of the goal drew as many cheers as the real thing.

That season Quinn handed over the coaching reins to new-comer Tom Renney. Although Renney's style was different from Ley's, he had no better luck. The team struggled all year, Pavel included. But it wasn't his surgically repaired knee that was giving him problems. In the first game of the season, Pavel had slid hard into the boards after being tripped. Although he continued to play, the impact had damaged his neck.

He finally left the lineup in March 1997, telling reporters, "It's my whole upper body—my neck, my chest, my spine, my arms, everything. I have pain 24 hours a day, even when I'm lying down. The last six weeks the pain has been awful." He didn't return for the rest of the season, and the team sank like a stone.

Prior to the 1997–98 season, the Canucks held two press conferences. The first was to reveal a new uniform featuring a killer-whale crest. The second was to announce they had signed free-agent center Mark Messier, one of hockey's legendary leaders, to a three-year us$20-million contract. Messier's appearance in a Canucks jersey created a surge of optimism, but it didn't last long.

To stop Pavel, defensemen have to play the body.

Just before the season began, the Vancouver newspapers reported that Pavel had asked to be traded. One of Pavel's agents, Serge Levin, confirmed the story. A few days later Pavel fired Salcer and Levin and dismissed Vladimir as his personal trainer. The split with his father was a serious one: they had stopped speaking entirely.

Pavel's new agent, Mike Gillis, met with Quinn to discuss the situation. When the season opened, Pavel was still a Canuck. Despite all its high-priced talent, the team performed poorly. After the club lost seven straight games, Quinn was fired as general manager and was replaced by a management committee. When the Canucks continued to lose, Renney was sent packing, too. He was replaced by Mike Keenan, Messier's former coach with the Rangers.

Keenan was known as a tough, demanding coach. At first it looked as if his harsh methods might succeed, but after a brief winning burst, the club slumped again. In January Keenan was given authority to make trades and began to clean house, trading fan favorites Trevor Linden, Kirk McLean, Martin Gelinas and Gino Odjick. By the season's end, Pavel was one of only four players left from the 1994 team that had gone to the Stanley Cup finals.

Despite the changes, the Canucks finished last in the Western Conference. Pavel's play was the lone bright light in a dark season. Healthy for the first time in three years, he scored 51 goals, one behind NHL leaders Teemu Selanne and Peter Bondra, and was third in scoring with 90 points. Vancouver fans voted Pavel the team's most valuable and most exciting player. But Canucks supporters who hoped the Russian Rocket had changed his mind about seeking a trade would be disappointed. He still wanted out.

OLYMPIC LIGHTNING

In February 1998, NHL players traveled to Japan to compete at the Winter Olympics for the first time. Pavel Bure captained the Russian team and had a brilliant tournament, scoring nine goals to lead all scorers, including five in one game against Finland. Although the Czech Republic and its star goalie Dominik Hasek defeated Russia 1–0 in the gold-medal game, Pavel made a lasting impression. Says hockey writer Roy MacGregor: "I have never seen anyone perform as well as Bure did that game. He didn't score, but he just seemed to be operating on a level above everyone else. Every time he touched the puck a jolt of electricity shot through the building."

In his first full season

with the Florida Panthers,

Pavel netted 58 goals

and set an incredible

21 team records.

CHAPTER FIVE

Miami Heat

During the summer, Pavel Bure decided the only way to force a trade was to refuse to play for Vancouver, even though he still had a year left on his contract. It was a headache newly hired Canucks general manager Brian Burke didn't need. "The reason for our reluctance to make a trade should be obvious to everyone," Burke said. "We go to sleep at night dreaming of getting players like Pavel Bure."

When nothing happened by the time the 1998–99 season started, Pavel flew home to Moscow. To stay in shape, he worked out on his own and practiced with his old team, Central Army. It wasn't until January 17 that Burke finally made a deal, sending his unhappy superstar to the Florida Panthers as part of a seven-player trade. The Panthers immediately inked Pavel to a huge five-year US$47.5-million contract.

After joining his new team in New York, Pavel gave an interview in which he explained his reasons for wanting to leave the Canucks. His problems, he claimed, were all with management, not with the city or its people. Even so, many Vancouver fans felt betrayed.

Because Pavel hadn't played in nine months, it was assumed he'd need at least a week to get in game shape. But the Muscovite was so eager that he suited up for a contest against the New York Islanders one day after his return. Although he played only 12 minutes, half his normal ice time, he scored twice in Florida's 5–2 win and was named the first star.

Pavel averages the most ice time of any NHL forward.

He scored again in his next game against the Rangers and then netted three against the Philadelphia Flyers. Florida's sluggish offense had suddenly caught fire. Said Panthers captain Scott Mellanby: "Bure's like a shark out there. Waiting, waiting, waiting—*boom*, he takes off."

When Pavel made his home debut with the Panthers on January 27, the club revved up the fans by showing a five-minute video of highlights from his career. The announcer then counted down from 10 and boomed, "The Russian Rocket has landed!" The crowd went crazy. Asked after the game for

his reaction to his trade and being back in the NHL, Pavel exclaimed, "It's a great feeling. I was missing this feeling."

In his first eight games with the Panthers, the Russian winger scored eight goals and three assists and caused an outburst of Pavelmania in the Sunshine State. After only a few weeks, Pavel had become the talk of Miami. But trouble loomed. On February 5, Pavel strained his knee in a game with the Pittsburgh Penguins. After sitting out for two weeks, he returned to play three more games and score five goals, but then left the lineup again. An examination revealed that the knee ligament he had torn in 1995 needed surgery once more. He would be sidelined for six months.

Some thought his career might be over. No NHLer had ever returned to play after two surgical reconstructions of the same knee. But Pavel stubbornly went to work rebuilding his damaged joint. By late summer he was back on skates. Panthers president Bill Torrey confidently stated: "I know what this guy is all about. He'll be back and he'll be every bit the player he was before."

In Florida's first game in 1999–2000, Pavel showed he hadn't lost his scoring touch, deflecting home a shot three minutes into the first period as the Panthers beat the Washington

Capitals 4–3. It took two months for Pavel to regain his form, but once he did he began filling the net. In December he rang up 12 goals and 10 assists to earn NHL player-of-the-month honors. By the All-Star break in February 2000, he had notched 44 points in his last 27 games and led the league with 37 goals.

Pavel was voted an All-Star by the fans for the fifth time in his career. Brother Valeri, who had been having a strong season with Calgary, also made the grade. Tatiana, the boys' mother, and Valeri's wife, actress Candace Cameron, flew into Toronto for the game. But Vladimir, who was still living in Vancouver, wasn't invited. In an interview, Vladimir said he had given everything up for his boys and now neither one would talk to him. He wouldn't watch the game. It was too painful.

The Bures played on a line with Viktor Kozlov of the Panthers. Pavel scored three times and added an assist, while Valeri had two helpers. Their total of six points broke the All-Star Game record by two brothers, set by Maurice and Henri Richard in 1958.

After the All-Star Game, Pavel continued his sizzling play. He finished the year with 58 goals, 14 more than the closest player, and won the Maurice "Rocket" Richard Trophy, awarded to the NHL's top

Russian Romance

In the winter of 1999, Pavel Bure began dating sexy Russian tennis star Anna Kournikova. Their relationship sparked gossip, not just because of their fame, but because Kournikova had also been dating Sergei Fedorov of the Detroit Red Wings. In February 2000, it was reported that Pavel had proposed marriage at a Miami restaurant and that Anna had accepted. News of their engagement made the front pages of all the Russian newspapers. But by April the couple had broken up. Within a few weeks Anna was back with Sergei.

goal scorer. Although Jaromir Jagr edged him out for the scoring title by two points, Pavel's performance had been astonishing. In all, he set an incredible 21 team records, and Florida had improved by 20 points to make the playoffs for the first time since 1997.

But the Panthers' season ended with a thud as they were swept by the New Jersey Devils in the first round. Vladimir Bure showed up for the series and told reporters he was rooting for New Jersey. He'd been hired by the Devils to work as trainer with several of the team's young players, including winger Scott Gomez, the eventual rookie of the year. When the Devils went on to win the Stanley Cup, Vladimir's name was engraved on the trophy with the rest of the team.

Despite their early playoff exit, the Panthers' leap in the standings inspired confidence. But instead of continuing to improve in 2000–01, Florida dive-bombed. Just after Christmas, coach Terry Murray and his brother, Bryan, the team's general manager, were both fired. Bill Torrey took over as GM and Duane Sutter was hired as the new coach.

Pavel on a breakaway is a goalie's worst nightmare.

Sutter increased Pavel's playing time, and the Russian Rocket responded by going on a scoring rampage. Unfortunately he was the club's only serious offensive threat, especially after Florida fell out of the playoff hunt and began trading its veterans. Despite a weak supporting cast, Pavel continued to score at a rapid clip, notching 59 goals to win his second straight Richard Trophy.

In the off-season, the Panthers acquired Valeri Bure from Calgary in a bid to pump up Florida's slumbering offense. But the club's problems couldn't be solved so easily. Both Bure brothers ran into injury problems in 2001–02 and Florida struggled badly. Early in December coach Duane Sutter was fired and replaced by Mike Keenan, and then in mid-March, with the team out of the playoff race, the Panthers traded Pavel to the New York Rangers for a package of players.

Pavel seemed thrilled by the move. He wore a broad smile when he met the Manhattan media at a press conference the next day. "It's great to be a part of the New York Rangers, one of the Original Six teams," he said. "It's been a dream of mine for a long time." He announced he would wear number 9 in New York as a tribute to his namesake, Maurice "Rocket" Richard. As Pavel explained, "Rocket Richard wore number 9. I won his trophy (for the NHL's top goal-scorer) twice. I think it's a good number."

Although New York failed to make the playoffs, Pavel looked terrific in Rangers blue, recording 20 points in 12 games and showing plenty of jump. His performance had Rangers fans eagerly looking forward to seeing what he could do over a full season. It's been said that the Russian Rocket plays his best hockey when he's on the big stage, and there aren't many bigger stages than the one at Madison Square Garden. Bure on Broadway: it sounds like a perfect match.

ONE-MAN BAND

No NHL player has ever supplied so much of his team's goal scoring as Pavel Bure did in 2000–01 with the Florida Panthers. The Russian sniper set a modern-day NHL record by notching 29.5 percent of the Florida Panthers' total goals.

Highest Percentage of a Team's Goals in a Season

Player	Year	Team	Goals	Team Goals	Pct.
Pavel Bure	2000–01	Florida	59	200	29.5
Brett Hull	1990–91	St. Louis	86	310	27.7
Jarome Iginla	2001–02	Calgary	52	201	25.9
Teemu Selanne	1997–98	Anaheim	52	205	25.4

STATISTICS

National Hockey League

Regular Season

Year	Team	GP	G	A	P	PIM
1991–92	Vancouver	65	34	26	60	30
1992–93	Vancouver	83	60	50	110	69
1993–94	Vancouver	76	60	47	107	86
1994–95	Vancouver	44	20	23	43	47
1995–96	Vancouver	15	6	7	13	8
1996–97	Vancouver	63	23	32	55	40
1997–98	Vancouver	82	51	39	90	48
1998–99	Florida	11	13	3	16	4
1999–00	Florida	74	58	36	94	16
2000–01	Florida	82	59	33	92	58
2001–02	Florida	56	22	27	49	56
	NY Rangers	12	12	8	20	6
Totals		**663**	**418**	**331**	**749**	**468**

Soviet Union/Russia

Year	Team	GP	G	A	P	PIM
1987–88	CSKA Moscow	5	1	1	2	0
1988–89	CSKA Moscow	32	17	9	26	8
1989–90	CSKA Moscow	46	14	10	24	20
1990–91	CSKA Moscow	44	35	11	46	24
1994–95	Spartak	1	2	0	2	2
Totals		**128**	**69**	**31**	**100**	**54**

Playoffs

Year	Team	GP	G	A	P	PIM
1991–92	Vancouver	13	6	4	10	14
1992–93	Vancouver	12	5	7	12	8
1993–94	Vancouver	24	16	15	31	40
1994–95	Vancouver	11	7	6	13	10
1999–00	Florida	4	1	3	4	2
Totals		**64**	**35**	**35**	**70**	**74**

International Hockey

Year	Event	GP	G	A	P	PIM
1989	World Juniors	7	8	6	14	4
1990	World Juniors	7	7	3	10	10
1990	World Championships	10	2	4	6	10
1991	World Championships	10	3	8	11	2
1998	Olympics	6	9	0	9	2
2000	World Championships	6	4	1	5	10
2002	Olympics	6	2	1	3	8
Totals		**52**	**35**	**23**	**58**	**46**

Key

GP = Games Played   G = Goals   A = Assists
P = Points   PIM = Penalties in Minutes